EXPLORE!

FORCE OF NATURE

T0419229

EARTHQUAKES

BY MONIKA DAVIES

Please visit our website, www.enslow.com. For a free color catalog of all our high-quality books, call toll free 1-800-398-2504 or fax 1-877-980-4454.

Cataloging-in-Publication Data

Names: Davies, Monika.
Title: Earthquakes / Monika Davies.
Description: New York : Enslow Publishing, 2021. | Series: Force of nature | Includes glossary and index.
Identifiers: ISBN 9781978518391 (pbk.) | ISBN 9781978518407 (library bound) | ISBN 9781978518414 (ebook)
Subjects: LCSH: Earthquakes–Juvenile literature. | Natural disasters–Juvenile literature.
Classification: LCC QE521.3 D383 2021 | DDC 551.22--dc23

Published in 2021 by
Enslow Publishing
101 West 23rd Street, Suite #240
New York, NY 10011

Copyright © 2021 Enslow Publishing

Designer: Katelyn E. Reynolds
Editor: Monika Davies

Photo credits: Cover, p. 1 Perfect Gui/Shutterstock.com; cover, pp. 1–48 (series art) Merfin/Shutterstock.com; p. 5 dailin/Shutterstock.com; p. 6 AFP via Getty Images; p. 7 Lukiyanova Natalia frenta/Shutterstock.com; pp. 8, 9 Designua/Shutterstock.com; p. 10 Lee Prince/Shutterstock.com; p. 11 Deni_Sugandi/Shutterstock.com; p. 12 Barks/Shutterstock.com; p. 13 Baron Wolman/The Image Bank/Getty Images Plus; pp. 14, 19 VectorMine/Shutterstock.com; pp. 15, 45 Christian Miranda/AFP via Getty Images; p. 17 Lloyd Cluff/Corbis Documentary/Getty Images Plus; pp. 18, 22 austinding/Shutterstock.com; p. 20 Ted Aljibe/AFP via Getty Images; p. 21 Renata Apanaviciene/Shutterstock.com; p. 23 Krista Abel/Shutterstock.com; p. 24 Doroniuk Anastasiia/Shutterstock.com; p. 25 Photography by Mangiwau/Moment/Getty Images; p. 27 © Corbis/Corbis via Getty Images; p. 28 Arnold Genthe/Getty Images; p. 29 Uwe Dedering/Wikipedia.org; p. 30 Juan Barreto/AFP via Getty Images; p. 31 Pascal Deloche/Corbis Documentary/Getty Images Plus; p. 32 Sunil Pradhan/NurPhoto/Getty Images; p. 33 Asanka Brendon Ratnayake/Lonely Planet Images/Getty Images Plus; p. 34 DigitalGlobe via Getty Images; p. 35 Satoshi Takahashi/LightRocket via Getty Images; p. 37 courtesy of the USGS; pp. 38, 39 Kimimasa Mayama/Bloomberg via Getty Images; p. 40 SpeedShutter/Shutterstock.com; p. 41 David McNew/Getty Images; p. 44 ChameleonsEye/Shutterstock.com.

Printed in the United States of America

Some of the images in this book illustrate individuals who are models. The depictions do not imply actual situations or events.

CPSIA compliance information: Batch #BS20ENS: For further information contact Enslow Publishing, New York, New York, at 1-800-542-2595.

Find us on

CONTENTS

WORDS IN THE GLOSSARY APPEAR IN **BOLD** TYPE THE FIRST TIME THEY ARE USED IN THE TEXT.

ALARMING QUAKES

Earthquakes are a truly unpredictable force of nature. These devastating natural disasters can cause intense ground shaking, **collapse** tall, multistory buildings, and crack open pavement. Earthquakes are often responsible for numerous deaths and injuries.

Scientists can guess the likelihood of an earthquake occurring in a certain area within a specific time frame. However, these predictions, or guesses, are not always accurate, or free from mistakes. This makes earthquakes unpredictable and therefore incredibly dangerous.

In this book, we'll look at how and why an earthquake happens, examine some of the most **destructive** earthquakes throughout history, and discuss how we can prepare for the earthquakes of the future.

ON MAY 12, 2008, A DEVASTATING EARTHQUAKE HIT THE SICHUAN PROVINCE IN CHINA. THE SICHUAN EARTHQUAKE OF 2008 LED TO NEARLY 90,000 DEATHS, AS WELL AS NEARLY 375,000 INJURIES. THE QUAKE DESTROYED AROUND 80 PERCENT OF BUILDINGS IN THE AREA, LEAVING MILLIONS OF PEOPLE HOMELESS.

UNEARTHING EARTHQUAKES

An earthquake is a shaking of the ground due to the sudden movement of rocks beneath Earth's surface. Earth's outer layer is called the crust. This rock shell ranges from about 3 to 44 miles (5 to 70 km) thick. The crust is the top part of a larger layer called the lithosphere. This layer is made of numerous large sections called plates. Earth's plates fit together like puzzle pieces.

A QUAKE CAN LAST FOR A FEW SECONDS, OR IT CAN LAST FOR SEVERAL MINUTES. IT MIGHT BE A LIGHT RUMBLE THAT YOU BARELY NOTICE, OR FURNITURE CAN MOVE AND OBJECTS CAN FALL OFF WALLS AND SHELVES. IN MORE SERIOUS QUAKES, THE GROUND CAN CRACK OPEN AND BUILDINGS CAN **TOPPLE**.

PLATE:

ONE OF THE LARGE PIECES OF ROCK THAT MAKE UP EARTH'S OUTER LAYER

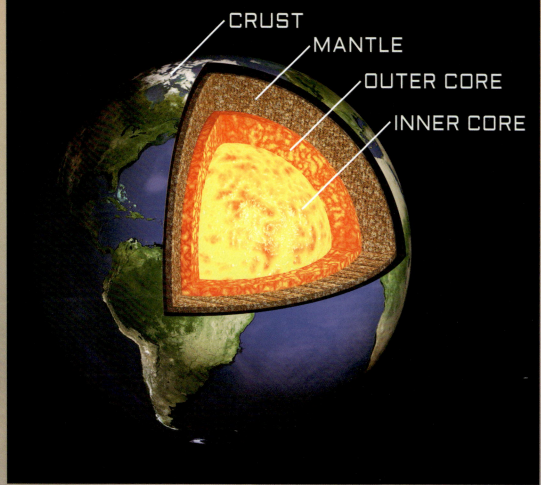

LOOK INSIDE THE EARTH

CRUST

MANTLE

OUTER CORE

INNER CORE

EARTH IS MADE OF FOUR MAJOR LAYERS: THE CRUST, THE MANTLE, THE OUTER CORE, AND THE INNER CORE.

The lithosphere "floats" on a layer of soft, hot rock. The plates can "drift" away from each other, leaving gaps. They can also push against each other, slide past one another, or slide under or over each other. These movements create tremendous pressure between the plates.

PRESSURE:
A FORCE THAT PUSHES ON SOMETHING ELSE

EARTH'S CONTINENTS

GEOLOGISTS, OR SCIENTISTS WHO STUDY EARTH AND ITS HISTORY, THINK THAT EARTH'S LAND WAS GROUPED INTO ONE "SUPERCONTINENT" CALLED PANGEA ABOUT 250 MILLION YEARS AGO. IT TOOK MILLIONS OF YEARS FOR THE PLATES MAKING UP THE SUPERCONTINENT TO DRIFT APART, IN TIME FORMING THE SEVEN CONTINENTS WE KNOW TODAY.

EARTH'S PLATES

Have you ever tried to stop someone bigger from getting past you? It probably wasn't easy. Earth's plates are very big, and they don't want to stop moving. Two plates create a lot of force when they crash into each other, slide past each other, or slide over or under each other. Different things can happen where two plates meet. One may slide under the other. Sometimes, plates fold under the pressure, rising up to make mountains. These movements don't happen quickly. Pressure builds up between plates over hundreds of years. When two plates suddenly slip and release this pressure, the energy let loose causes an earthquake.

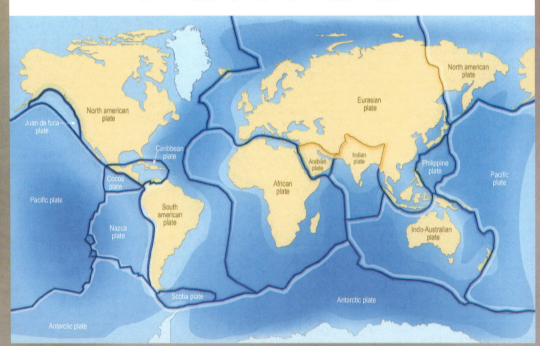

TECTONIC PLATES

THIS MAP SHOWS EARTH'S MAJOR AND MINOR PLATES. THERE ARE ABOUT 15 TO 20 TECTONIC PLATES, OR MOVEABLE MASSES OF ROCK, THAT MAKE UP EARTH'S CRUST.

A fault is a fracture, or break, in Earth's crust. A fault occurs when two sections of crust slip and move by each other. The **boundaries** between plates are faults. Faults can also form farther away from these boundaries.

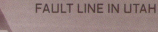 FAULT LINE IN UTAH

MOST EARTHQUAKES AND MOST VOLCANOES OCCUR ALONG THE BOUNDARIES BETWEEN TECTONIC PLATES. EARTHQUAKES OCCUR AT THESE BOUNDARIES BECAUSE OF THE MOVEMENT OF PLATES. VOLCANOES OCCUR AT THESE BOUNDARIES BECAUSE THEY ALLOW MAGMA TO RISE TO EARTH'S SURFACE.

EXPLORE MORE

VOLCANOES FORM WHEN MAGMA, OR LIQUID ROCK FROM THE MANTLE, RISES TO EARTH'S SURFACE. THAT CAN HAPPEN WHEN ONE PLATE SLIDES UNDER ANOTHER. THE SINKING PLATE CARRIES WATER WITH IT, AND THE HEAT INSIDE EARTH CAUSES IT TO BOIL, WHICH MELTS ROCK THAT RISES TO THE SURFACE.

11

There are three main kinds of faults. A normal fault occurs when one block of Earth's crust slides down and away from another block. A **reverse** fault occurs when two blocks compress together, causing one block to push up and over the other block. Both normal and reverse faults result in one block rising up higher than the other. A strike-slip fault occurs when two blocks move **horizontally** in opposite directions.

During an earthquake, the pressure between two plates is released suddenly. This sends out vibrations, or waves of energy, in all directions. Geologists call these vibrations seismic waves. There are two kinds of seismic waves: body waves and surface waves.

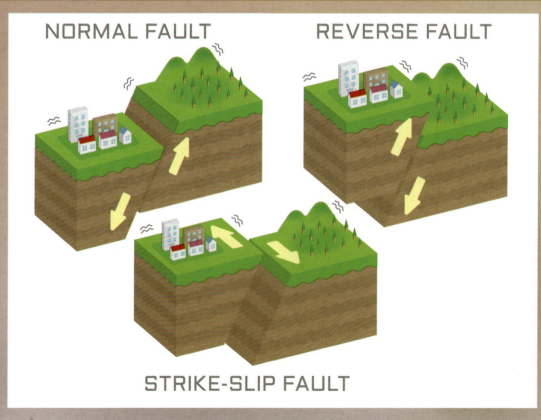

NORMAL FAULT

REVERSE FAULT

STRIKE-SLIP FAULT

EXPLORE MORE

THE PACIFIC PLATE AND THE NORTH AMERICAN PLATE MEET TO FORM A STRIKE-SLIP FAULT THAT RUNS THROUGH THE STATE OF CALIFORNIA. THE SAN ANDREAS FAULT IS ABOUT 800 MILES (1,287 KM) LONG.

MAJOR EARTHQUAKES OCCUR ALONG THE SAN ANDREAS FAULT LINE ONCE EVERY 150 TO 200 YEARS.

13

Body waves move from the fault slip toward Earth's surface. Primary body waves (or P waves) move the fastest. They travel through land and water, pushing and pulling as they go. Secondary body waves (or S waves) are slower. They can't travel through water. They move from side to side. Surface waves travel across Earth's surface. They cause the most **damage** because they move the ground up and down and side to side.

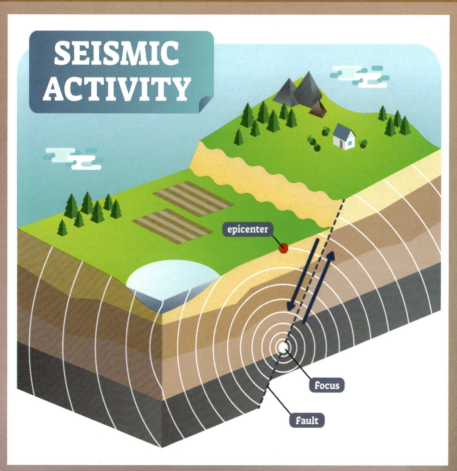

SEISMIC ACTIVITY

epicenter

focus

fault

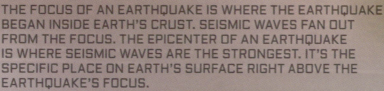

THE FOCUS OF AN EARTHQUAKE IS WHERE THE EARTHQUAKE BEGAN INSIDE EARTH'S CRUST. SEISMIC WAVES FAN OUT FROM THE FOCUS. THE EPICENTER OF AN EARTHQUAKE IS WHERE SEISMIC WAVES ARE THE STRONGEST. IT'S THE SPECIFIC PLACE ON EARTH'S SURFACE RIGHT ABOVE THE EARTHQUAKE'S FOCUS.

SEISMOLOGY

Seismology is the study of earthquakes and seismic waves. Scientists called seismologists concentrate on many areas of research. Some use seismic waves to **calculate** the earthquake's focus. Others calculate the magnitude of earthquakes. Seismologists may also collect data, or facts and figures, that expand knowledge about the specific **hazards** of earthquakes. They might examine why and how earthquakes begin, as well as where the next one might happen. They're also able to use seismic waves from earthquakes to get an idea of what the inside of Earth looks like and build models that show Earth's structure.

SEISMOLOGISTS MAY WORK AT OBSERVATORIES OR ANALYSIS CENTERS. GOVERNMENTS AND UNIVERSITIES USUALLY FUND THESE OBSERVATORIES AND CENTERS.

MAGNITUDE:
A MEASURE OF THE POWER OF AN EARTHQUAKE

QUAKE STRENGTH

Earthquakes can be so strong they change the way Earth looks. They can change a river's course, create valleys, and raise mountains. They can have harmful effects on the places where people live. Strong earthquakes can damage or destroy property. They can injure or kill people and animals.

Earthquake damage depends on several things. An earthquake's magnitude plays a large role in the amount of destruction it causes. The farther away from an earthquake's focus, the weaker the tremors will be. The type of soil or rock found in the location where an earthquake hits also has an effect on how much damage it causes.

RESEARCHERS HAVE DISCOVERED IF GROUND IS MADE OF SOFT SOIL, IT'LL EXPERIENCE GREATER SHAKING AND SHIFTING DURING AN EARTHQUAKE.

TREMOR:
A SHAKING MOVEMENT CAUSED BY AN EARTHQUAKE

17

Earthquakes, especially the stronger ones, often occur in a series. The earthquake with the greatest magnitude in the series is called the mainshock. A small earthquake is sometimes a sign that a stronger one will follow. An earthquake that comes before the mainshock is called a foreshock.

SERIES:
A NUMBER OF EVENTS THAT OCCUR ONE AFTER THE OTHER

THE GREATER THE MAGNITUDE OF AN EARTHQUAKE, THE MORE DESTRUCTION IT CAN CAUSE.

MEASURING MAGNITUDE

Scientists use several scales to measure the magnitude of earthquakes. In the past, the most common scale used was the Richter scale. Charles F. Richter created this scale in 1935, which used a mathematical formula to measure and compare the size of earthquakes. Nowadays, scientists use a different formula, known as the moment magnitude scale, to calculate the size and strength of earthquakes. The formula uses all of the earthquake's different seismic waves, leading to more exact measurements compared to the Richter scale. Using these measurements, earthquakes are sorted into a class, or group. Each whole number in the moment magnitude scale represents a magnitude 10 times more powerful than the whole number before it.

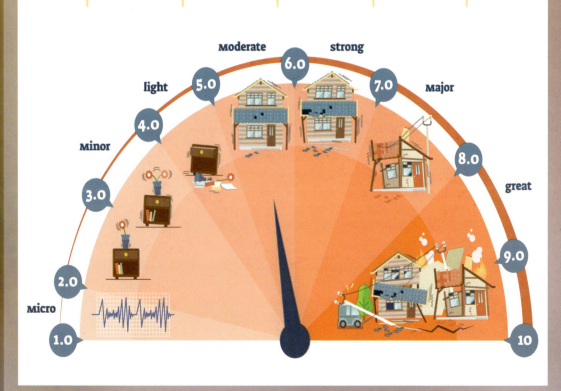

EARTHQUAKE MAGNITUDE SCALE

micro 1.0
2.0
minor 3.0
4.0
light 5.0
moderate 6.0
strong 7.0 major
8.0 great
9.0
10

AN EARTHQUAKE IS CONSIDERED "MAJOR" WHEN ITS MAGNITUDE IS MEASURED AT 7.0 OR HIGHER. A MAJOR EARTHQUAKE CAUSES MASSIVE DESTRUCTION AND OFTEN MANY DEATHS.

Strong earthquakes are commonly followed by many earthquakes of lesser magnitude. These are called aftershocks. Aftershocks are the result of Earth's crust settling into place. Each aftershock is less powerful than the one that came before it. However, aftershocks can be as dangerous as the mainshock and can contribute to damage.

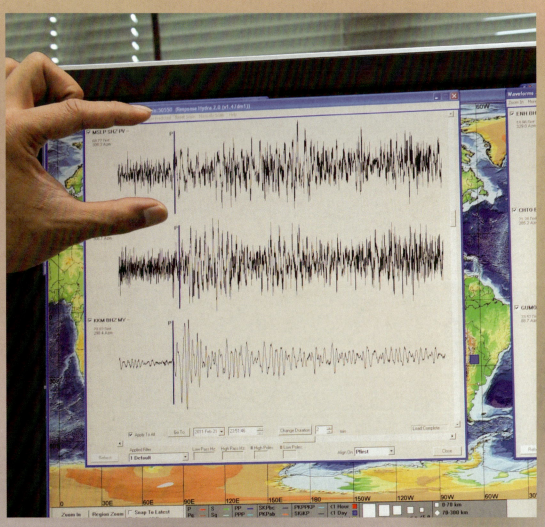

SCIENTISTS USE SEISMOGRAPHS, OR SEISMOMETERS, TO FIGURE OUT HOW STRONG AN EARTHQUAKE IS AND HOW LONG IT LASTS. A SEISMOGRAPH OR SEISMOMETER IS AN INSTRUMENT THAT MEASURES AND RECORDS THE SHAKING GROUND DURING AN EARTHQUAKE.

MINING, OR THE ACT OF DIGGING SOMETHING OUT OF THE GROUND, IS ONE OF THE LEADING CAUSES OF MAN-MADE EARTHQUAKES.

EXPLORE MORE

NOT ALL EARTHQUAKES ARE CAUSED BY NATURAL PROCESSES. SOME ARE CAUSED BY PEOPLE. THE WEIGHT OF MAN-MADE LAKES BEHIND LARGE DAMS CAN ALSO SET OFF EARTHQUAKES. MILITARIES HAVE CAUSED EARTHQUAKES BY TESTING **NUCLEAR** WEAPONS UNDERGROUND.

Strong earthquakes that strike populated areas cause great destruction. Buildings, bridges, and other structures break and fall. People are harmed and sometimes trapped by falling debris. Tremors may also destroy roads and railroads. The ground may even crack open and seem to swallow cars and buildings!

EARTHQUAKE FACT FILE

Did you know there's likely an earthquake happening right now? Every day, several hundred earthquakes occur, many of them too small for people to notice. These earthquakes measure at magnitude 2.0 or smaller. The U.S. Geological Survey (USGS) estimates there are 500,000 **detectable** earthquakes every year. People feel the effects of 100,000 of these earthquakes, while only 100 will cause actual damage. In the United States, Alaska is the state most likely to experience an earthquake. Florida and North Dakota are the two states that experience the least number of earthquakes.

IN CALIFORNIA, A SEICHE (SAYSH) IS A COMMON SIGHT IN SWIMMING POOLS DURING AND AFTER AN EARTHQUAKE. A SEICHE IS WHEN WATER SLOSHES, OR MOVES IN A MESSY WAY, WITHIN A CLOSED BODY OF WATER.

Earthquakes can create landslides. The moving masses of rock and earth can cover or even destroy homes, roads, and other structures. Strong earthquakes at sea cause giant waves called tsunamis. When tsunamis hit land, they flood cities and towns, knock down structures, and drown people. Severe tremors can make soil loose, causing structures to topple.

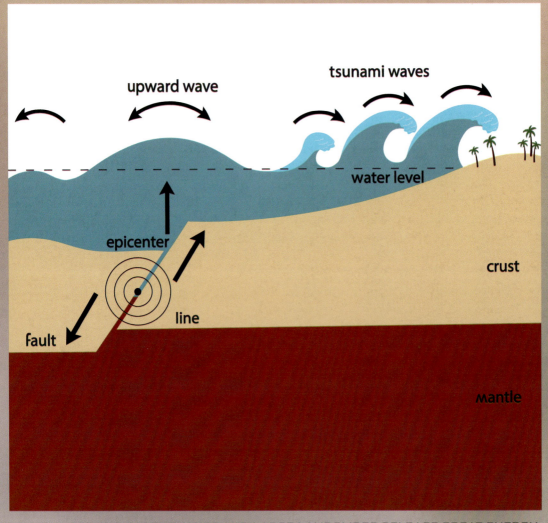

STRONG EARTHQUAKES AND LARGE LANDSLIDES RELEASE GREAT ENERGY THAT CAN MOVE, OR DISPLACE, A LOT OF WATER. WHILE THE FORCE OF THE ENERGY PUSHES THE WATER UP, GRAVITY PULLS IT DOWN. THIS CAUSES WAVES TO SPREAD IN ALL DIRECTIONS.

LANDSLIDE:
THE SUDDEN MOVEMENT OF ROCKS AND DIRT DOWN A HILL OR MOUNTAIN

EXPLORE MORE

ON DECEMBER 26, 2004, A 9.1 MAGNITUDE EARTHQUAKE ON THE BOTTOM OF THE INDIAN OCEAN CREATED A TSUNAMI. GIANT WAVES HAMMERED SEVERAL COUNTRIES. THE ISLAND OF SUMATRA GOT HIT THE WORST. WAVES TRAVELED AS FAR AS 3,000 MILES (4,800 KM), STRIKING AFRICA.

MORE THAN 200,000 PEOPLE DIED IN THE INDIAN OCEAN TSUNAMI, MAKING IT THE DEADLIEST TSUNAMI ON RECORD. THIS PHOTOGRAPH, TAKEN EIGHT MONTHS AFTER THE NATURAL DISASTER, SHOWS THE AFTERMATH OF THE TSUNAMI.

HISTORIC EARTHQUAKES

The deadliest earthquake in U.S. history occurred near the city of San Francisco in 1906. The earthquake was the result of rupturing in the northern section of the San Andreas fault. After just 60 seconds of tremors, San Francisco—as well as other parts of California—experienced incredible amounts of damage. Altogether, more than 28,000 buildings were destroyed. Out of a population of about 400,000, about 225,000 people were left homeless.

Some described the sound of the earthquake as similar to "the roar of 10,000 lions." The quake was felt in both Californita and Nevada.

THIS PHOTOGRAPH SHOWS SAN FRANCISCO AFTER THE DEVASTATING 1906 EARTHQUAKE.

RUPTURE:
A CRACK OR BREAK IN SOMETHING

The 1906 earthquake in San Francisco started fires that swept through the city for three days. About 3,000 people died as a result of the 1906 earthquake. Shortly after, scientists began studying the San Andreas fault. This marked the beginning of modern earthquake study in the United States.

THE FIRES THAT BLAZED THROUGH SAN FRANCISCO RUINED ALMOST 500 BLOCKS IN THE CITY CENTER. ACCORDING TO A NATIONAL OCEANIC AND ATMOSPHERIC ADMINISTRATION (NOAA) REPORT, IT'S ESTIMATED THE EARTHQUAKE CAUSED MORE THAN $400 MILLION WORTH OF PROPERTY DAMAGE.

THE SHAANXI EARTHQUAKE

The deadliest earthquake on record occurred in the two provinces of Shaanxi and Shanxi, China, in 1556. About 830,000 people died. It's believed the huge number of deaths led to the population in the area to decline by 60 percent. At that time, many people in the region lived in man-made caves cut into cliffs. Most of these dwellings were destroyed. The quake also opened up giant cracks in the ground and started landslides that killed many people. Following the earthquake, people began building structures with materials that would be more resistant to earthquakes, including bamboo and wood.

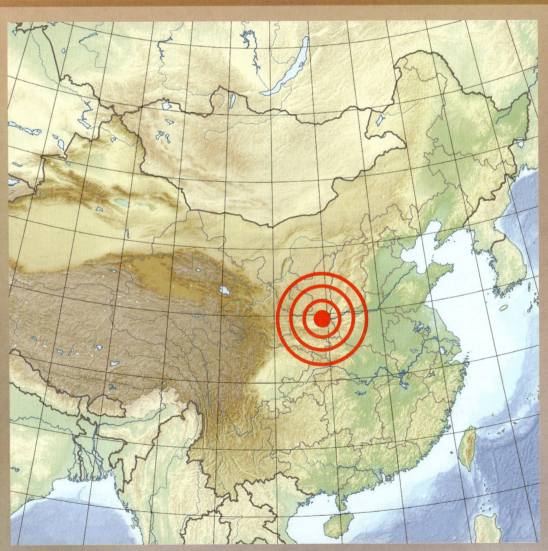

THIS MAP SHOWS THE EPICENTER OF THE SHAANXI EARTHQUAKE. THE EPICENTER WAS NEAR THE CITY OF HUAXIAN IN THE SHAANXI PROVINCE.

On January 12, 2010, a 7.0 magnitude earthquake struck just 15 miles (25 km) southwest of Port-au-Prince, Haiti. The focus wasn't very deep. It was just 8.1 miles (13 km) beneath Earth's surface, which increased the damage it caused. Over the next several weeks, many aftershocks occurred. Fifty-nine aftershocks were greater than 4.5 on the Richter scale. Two of them were 5.9 and 6.0 in magnitude.

Poor building standards in Haiti resulted in massive damage. Buildings crumbled, trapping and killing many people. Over 200,000 buildings were damaged or destroyed. It's estimated that more than 220,000 people died, 300,000 were injured, and around 1.5 million people were left homeless.

THE SHOCKS OF THE 2010 EARTHQUAKE WERE MOST STRONGLY FELT IN HAITI AND THE DOMINICAN REPUBLIC. HOWEVER, THE EARTHQUAKE ALSO SHOOK AREAS IN CUBA, JAMAICA, AND PUERTO RICO.

THRUST FAULT:
A BREAK OR FAULT THAT OCCURS WHEN ONE BLOCK OF EARTH'S CRUST MOVES UP AND OVER ANOTHER BLOCK

EXPLORE MORE

THE 2010 HAITI EARTHQUAKE WAS CAUSED BY A PREVIOUSLY UNKNOWN FAULT. SCIENTISTS CALL IT THE LÉOGÂNE FAULT AFTER A HAITIAN TOWN DIRECTLY OVER IT. THE FRACTURE IS A TYPE OF REVERSE FAULT KNOWN AS A THRUST FAULT.

PORT-AU-PRINCE, HAITI

31

2015 NEPAL EARTHQUAKE

On April 25, 2015, a magnitude 7.8 earthquake hit central Nepal, killing around 9,000 people and injuring thousands more. The earthquake's epicenter was around 48 miles (77 km) from Kathmandu, the capital city of Nepal. The earthquake, as well as its aftershocks, led to several landslides that destroyed small villages, as well as parts of Kathmandu. The city suffered a great deal of damage from the quake, and many historical buildings in the city's center were demolished, or destroyed. A UN (United Nations) report found that the lives of more than 8 million people were impacted by this earthquake.

THE 2015 NEPAL EARTHQUAKE WAS RESPONSIBLE FOR DAMAGING OR DESTROYING MORE THAN 600,000 BUILDINGS, INCLUDING MULTISTORY STRUCTURES IN KATHMANDU.

THERE WERE HUNDREDS OF AFTERSHOCKS FOLLOWING THE MAIN QUAKE IN NEPAL.

On March 11, 2011, a 9.0 magnitude earthquake occurred off the northeastern coast of Japan. It was the most destructive earthquake in the country's history. Several foreshocks struck in the days before the mainshock, and hundreds of aftershocks followed. Soon after the earthquake, a tsunami hit the coast. Together, the earthquake and the tsunami killed more than 14,000 people. Seven weeks after the disaster, 13,000 people were still missing.

THE TSUNAMI STRUCK THE FUKUSHIMA DAIICHI NUCLEAR POWER STATION, WHICH SUFFERED MAJOR DAMAGE. THE POWER STATION CAUGHT ON FIRE, AND RADIOACTIVE FUEL LEAKED INTO THE OCEAN AND AIR.

RADIOACTIVE:
PUTTING OUT HARMFUL ENERGY IN THE FORM OF TINY PARTICLES

EXPLORE MORE

ONE JAPANESE TOWN ESCAPED THE TSUNAMI'S EFFECTS, THANKS TO A PAST LEADER. KOTAKU WAMURA, FORMER MAYOR OF FUDAI, SAW A TSUNAMI DESTROY HIS TOWN IN 1933. WAMURA HAD A LARGE WALL BUILT TO PROTECT THE TOWN WHEN HE WAS MAYOR. TODAY, THE PEOPLE OF FUDAI ARE GRATEFUL FOR HIS EFFORTS.

MANY TOWNS IN JAPAN WERE LEVELED BY THE EARTHQUAKE IN 2011.

35

PREPARING FOR THE FUTURE

After years of studying earthquakes, scientists still can't predict when and where they'll occur. However, they can predict where one is likely to occur based on previous earthquakes, the movement of plates, and the positions of fault lines.

Scientists can also give a general idea of when a quake might occur. For example, if an area has had four large earthquakes in the past 200 years, scientists will say there is a 50 percent chance of another large earthquake in the next 50 years. In the end, predictions can't give us an exact idea of where and when an earthquake may happen.

PREDICT:
TO GUESS WHAT WILL HAPPEN IN THE FUTURE BASED ON FACTS OR KNOWLEDGE

NATIONAL SEISMIC HAZARD MAP

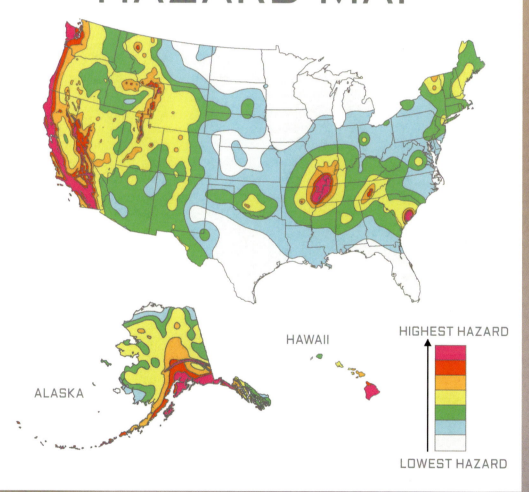

HIGHEST HAZARD

LOWEST HAZARD

ALASKA

HAWAII

THIS 2014 USGS NATIONAL SEISMIC HAZARD MAP SHOWS THE LIKELIHOOD OF DIFFERENT LEVELS OF EARTHQUAKE SHAKING HAPPENING THROUGHOUT THE UNITED STATES. AREAS WITH A HIGHER HAZARD LEVEL ARE MORE LIKELY TO EXPERIENCE EARTHQUAKES, WHICH ARE ALSO MORE LIKELY TO BE DESTRUCTIVE IN NATURE.

Since the 1906 San Francisco quake, earthquake preparations have advanced. Structures built where earthquakes commonly occur are stronger than they once were. Some are even built to sway during a quake instead of break.

AFTER THE 2011 EARTHQUAKE IN JAPAN, BUILDERS LOOKED FOR WAYS TO MAKE BUILDINGS SAFER DURING EARTHQUAKES.

EXPLORE MORE

ONE OF THE MOST IMPORTANT WAYS TO KEEP PEOPLE SAFE DURING AN EARTHQUAKE IS A **PREVENTIVE** MEASURE: BUILD EARTHQUAKE-RESISTANT BUILDINGS. ONE WAY THAT BUILDINGS ARE BUILT TO BE EARTHQUAKE RESISTANT IS TO HAVE THEM HAVE A SYMMETRICAL DESIGN. THIS MEANS THE DIFFERENT SIDES OF THE BUILDING ARE THE SAME.

CAN ANIMALS PREDICT EARTHQUAKES?

Throughout history, there have been reports of animals acting strangely before earthquakes. Ancient Greek historians recorded that in 373 BCE, rats, snakes, and weasels fled the city of Helike days before an earthquake struck. Some stories suggest that the common toad can predict earthquakes too. Some researchers think certain animals can feel or sense seismic waves, which may be why they flee or act oddly before a quake begins. However, many reports of animals acting strangely prior to an earthquake are simply based on observations by people. For now, there's no clear proof from long-term research studies that animals can predict earthquakes.

THE MATERIALS USED TO BUILD A STRUCTURE ARE ALSO IMPORTANT WHEN IT COMES TO EARTHQUAKE-RESISTANT BUILDINGS. FOR EXAMPLE, BRICK BUILDINGS ARE LESS ABLE TO BEND AND SHIFT WHEN AN EARTHQUAKE STRIKES, MAKING THEM MORE LIKELY TO FALL. BUT BUILDINGS MADE OF STRUCTURAL STEEL ARE MORE ABLE TO BEND WITHOUT BREAKING DURING A QUAKE.

If you live where earthquakes occur, there's a lot you and your family can do to be prepared for a quake. Keep an emergency kit with drinking water, food, flashlights, fire extinguishers, and first aid supplies in your home. Know how to shut off the gas, electricity, and water in case the lines break. Secure refrigerators and water heaters to walls to stop them from falling over. Store breakables on low shelves. Practice how to stay safe during an earthquake.

HAVING AN EARTHQUAKE PREPAREDNESS KIT COULD SAVE YOUR LIFE!

THIS PHOTOGRAPH SHOWS STUDENTS PRACTICING EARTHQUAKE SAFETY. TO PROTECT THEMSELVES FROM FALLING OBJECTS, THEY USE ONE ARM TO COVER THEIR HEAD AND NECK. THEY USE THEIR OTHER ARM TO HOLD ON TO A STURDY OBJECT.

EXPLORE MORE

REMEMBER THE MAINSHOCK OF AN EARTHQUAKE IS USUALLY FOLLOWED BY AFTERSHOCKS. AFTERSHOCKS MAY CAUSE DAMAGED BUILDINGS TO FULLY COLLAPSE. AFTER THE MAINSHOCK OF A QUAKE, MAKE SURE TO LEAVE ANY PARTIALLY DAMAGED BUILDING IN CASE THERE ARE AFTERSHOCKS.

EARTHQUAKE SAFETY

IF YOU'RE INDOORS:

- HIDE UNDER A HEAVY TABLE OR DESK
- STAY AWAY FROM WINDOWS
- STAY AWAY FROM WALLS THAT MAY FALL
- DON'T USE ELEVATORS
- DON'T RUN OUTSIDE BECAUSE YOU MIGHT GET HIT BY FALLING DEBRIS

DEBRIS:
THE REMAINS OF SOMETHING THAT HAS BEEN BROKEN

42

IF YOU'RE OUTSIDE:

- RUN TO AN OPEN AREA AWAY FROM BUILDINGS, TREES, AND POWER LINES

- DON'T RUN INTO A BUILDING

IF YOU'RE IN A CAR:

- STOP AS QUICKLY AND SAFELY AS YOU CAN

- STAY IN THE CAR

- STEER CLEAR OF BUILDINGS, TREES, POWER LINES, AND BRIDGES

Earthquakes destroy property and claim lives. Although scientists try to predict where and when they'll happen, it's not easy. Every year, earthquakes affect people around the world. They're frightening forces of nature capable of causing serious and deadly damage. However, knowing what to do during a quake will help you stay alive. While earthquakes are a deadly force of nature, there are ways people can stay safe during and after these devastating natural disasters.

EVACUATION MEANS TO WITHDRAW FROM A PLACE FOR PROTECTION. IF YOU LIVE IN AN AREA WHERE EARTHQUAKES OCCUR, IT'S IMPORTANT TO KNOW YOUR EARTHQUAKE EVACUATION ROUTE. YOUR EVACUATION ROUTE MAY CHANGE FOR DIFFERENT NATURAL DISASTERS!

THE EFFECTS OF CLIMATE CHANGE

Climate change has led directly to an increase in global temperatures. In particular, climate change has led to ocean surface temperatures increasing, as well as higher sea levels. There is evidence that climate change will lead to stronger and more intense **hurricanes**, or typhoons. A 2009 study in Taiwan examined a link between typhoons with small earthquakes happening under the island. The study found typhoons could lead to higher stress, or pressure, on fault lines. This could then cause an earthquake. However, while there is direct evidence climate change will likely lead to more severe hurricanes, blizzards, and other natural disasters, there is no long-term evidence that climate change will lead to more earthquakes or increase the intensity of earthquakes.

CLIMATE CHANGE:
LONG-TERM CHANGE IN EARTH'S CLIMATE, CAUSED PARTLY BY HUMAN ACTIVITIES SUCH AS BURNING OIL AND NATURAL GAS

SCIENTISTS AROUND THE WORLD WILL KEEP STUDYING EARTHQUAKES TO GET BETTER AT UNDERSTANDING THEIR CAUSES AND PREDICTING WHEN THEY MAY HAPPEN.

GLOSSARY

boundary Something that marks the limit of an area or place.

calculate To figure something out using math.

collapse To fall down or cave in.

damage Harm; also, to cause harm.

destructive Causing damage or ruin.

detectable Able to be noticed or discovered.

hazard A source of danger.

horizontally In a manner level with the line that seems to form where Earth meets the sky.

hurricane A powerful storm that forms over water.

nuclear Having to do with the power created by splitting atoms, the smallest bits of matter.

preventive Used to stop something bad from occurring.

reverse To move in the opposite direction.

topple To fall forward or tip over.

FOR MORE INFORMATION

BOOKS

Hanel, Rachael. *Can You Survive an Earthquake? An Interactive Survival Adventure*. Mankato, MN: Capstone Press, 2013.

Stark, Kristy. *Predicting Earthquakes*. Huntington Beach, CA: Teacher Created Materials, 2018.

Tarshis, Lauren. *I Survived the San Francisco Earthquake, 1906*. New York, NY: Scholastic, 2012.

Van Rose, Susanna. *DK Eyewitness: Volcano & Earthquake*. New York, NY: DK Publishing, 2014.

WEBSITES

Earthquakes
www.dkfindout.com/uk/earth/earthquakes
Discover more about where and why earthquakes occur.

Earthquakes for Kids
earthquake.usgs.gov/learn/kids
Learn more about earthquakes and see the latest quakes here.

What Is an Earthquake?
spaceplace.nasa.gov/earthquakes/en
Find out how we measure earthquakes and if earthquakes happen only on Earth at this site.

INDEX